CW00376601

IS THIS ABOUT ME OR YOU?

How highly effective leaders
listen, understand and respond
to people who are upset

ANDREW PRIESTLEY

WM

Is This About Me Or You?

First published in June 2020

ISBN 978-1-912774-58-6

Andrew Priestley

The rights of Andrew Priestley to be identified as contributing author of this work has been asserted in accordance with Sections 77 and 78 of the Copyright Designs and Patents Act, 1988.

A CIP catalogue record for this book is available from the British Library.

All rights reserved. No part of this book may be reproduced in material (including photocopying or storing in any medium by electronic means and whether or not transiently or incidentally to some other use of this publication) without the written permission of the copyright holder except in accordance with the provisions of the Copyright, design and Patents Act 1988. Applications for the Copyright holders written permission to reproduce any part of this publication should be addressed to the publisher.

Disclaimer: *Is This About Me Or You?* is intended for information and education purposes only. This book does not constitute specific legal, financial, clinical or commercial advice unique to your situation.

The views and opinions expressed in this book are those of the authors and do not reflect those of the Publisher and Resellers, who accept no responsibility for loss, damage or injury to persons or their belongings as a direct or indirect result of reading this book.

All people mentioned in case studies have been used with permission, and/or have had names, genders, industries and personal details altered to protect client confidentiality. Any resemblance to persons living or dead is purely coincidental.

Contents

Is This About Me Or You?

At A Glance

When we're communicating - chatting face-to-face, by phone, in meetings, writing, emailing - words and ideas get exchanged. This book is about face-to-face communication, specifically, the times when you sense the energy and tone of the exchange has somehow shifted from a neutral to a more adversarial position.

So for this entire book I will be using the diagram in the Appendix. It maps the typical milestones we can observe in difficult professional and personal exchanges

This is an incredibly simple and elegant conflict management model that I've taught to hundreds of leaders world wide ... that works.

Keep it simple, too.

Words And Ideas Are Exchanging

So when we communicate, words and ideas are being exchanged. Normally, what will happen is you'll be talking to someone and words and ideas are simply being exchanged. Back and forth. To and fro.

Senders. Receivers.

Talking. Listening.

And the best interactions have a sense that you're enjoying the exchange. And I want to emphasise a sense that there's no problem underlying that exchange of words and ideas.

We're just freely exchanging words and ideas.

I'm sure you've probably had lots of conversations where you have a good dialogue with someone, and you come away with a *sense* of having had a *good conversation*.

A good exchange. Right?

There's no negative residue. No bad feelings. No self talk or chatter. No after-burn. Nothing.

You might be reflecting on what was exchanged, sure, but there's no sense of angst. Or frustration. Or a sense of *What did they mean by that? Why did they say that?* No agenda.

It was all constructive. Positive. Normal. OK.

Do you know what I'm saying?

But there's some point ... in some conversations where words and ideas are exchanging ... you're listening to what is being said and ... something changes. There's a gear change.

Energetically, it *feels* something happened. You hear a problem. In truth, you *feel* a problem.

What was that they just said? Really? You're now sensing a problem.

Importantly, you *feel* it. You feel the energy has shifted. You *feel* it inside your body. Or you have a thought. Then suddenly you're listening is different. *What did they just say? Why? Why did they just say that?*

And this can be rapid. Extremely rapid.

But you *feel* it. It registers. It gets your attention. It suddenly *feels* different. And if you suddenly find yourself reacting, then something did change.

If that happens, you took it personally. You made it about you.

Does this sound familiar?

Part 1

This Is About Me

Now I'm Hearing A Problem

You're chatting with someone. Talking. Listening. And suddenly ... you sense a problem.

It can be a *direct* comment ... or *indirect*.

Here's the **direct** version.

I was in a meeting chatting about a client issue and my colleague says, *No. I disagree. That is the WRONG way to handle this situation, because ...* .

Now, I am OK with people not agreeing with me. I don't usually feel defensive about a disagreement. But it was the *way* he said it.

NO ... I disagree ... that is THE WRONG WAY to handle this.

What I heard was: *YOU ... ARE HANDLING THIS WRONG ... YOU ARE WRONG.*

Now there's a problem.

This suddenly became personal.

In my mind, my professionalism, my skills, and capabilities are being questioned. Well, that's what I am now thinking anyway. And I'm now feeling defensive. Criticised. Attacked. And I am preparing to push back.

Has this ever happened to you?

Here's the **indirect** version. You get a lot of this type because a lot of people don't say what they mean or mean what they say.

I was in a meeting chatting about a client issue and my colleague, suddenly, out of nowhere says, *No tie today?*

And immediately ... *immediately* ... I think: *What? What does he mean by 'No tie today'? Where did that come from? What's wrong with 'no tie'? Why did he say that? What's that about?*

What I heard was ... *YOU LOOK UNPROFESSIONAL.*

Now there's a problem.

This suddenly became personal. Now my professionalism, my skills, and capabilities ... *and now my dress sense* ... are being questioned.

Well, that's what I am now thinking, anyway.

And I feel defensive. Criticised. Attacked. And I am now preparing to push back.

I don't care what it was about. Somebody said something ... and you immediately (or later) felt nudged ... or pushed off centre.

Chipped. Chided. Undermined. Devalued. Questioned.

Has *this* ever happened to you?

Two Filters

What just happened is you filtered the message. Because humans are meaning-making organisms, you most likely *added meaning* to what was said.

But the message got filtered.

Especially when the conversation has a subtle or obvious change in emotional energy. There are lots of filters but I only want to deal with two in this book.

The message either goes down a filter called, **This about me** or **This about you.** It looks like this.

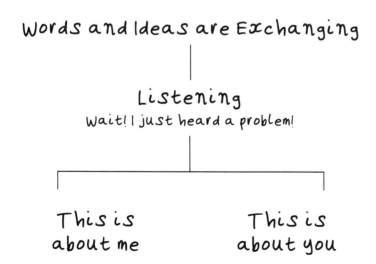

Words and Ideas are Exchanging

Listening
Wait! I just heard a problem!

This is about me

This is about you

Whichever filter you choose is highly predictive of what happens next.

Either, the chance for misunderstanding is going to increase and the conversation is going to stall, stop or deteriorate ... *and* potentially, things will escalate and get worse ... and lead to conflict.

Or potentially, you will reach a greater understand more quickly and the potential for conflict will diminish and diffuse ... or not even happen, at all.

Your choice.

This Is About Me

So ...

... what happens if the message goes down the *This is about me* filter? (And that can happen rapidly.)

In most cases, if you hear something that sounds like a problem - like a criticism - then your initial reaction is most likely to be: *shock*.

This about me!

So, I'm in a business meeting ... and I'm not wearing a tie. And my colleague says, *No tie today?*

And I think, *What the ... ? He's having a shot at me! He is having a crack at me for not wearing a tie!*

My listening went from words and ideas are being positively exchanged to now I'm hearing a problem. There's a problem here. *And this is about me.*

That's how you interpret it. There's a problem. *And it's about me.* I think it's directed at me. It's aimed at me.

And, by the way, it will show up as a feeling a lot sooner than the words show up.

You *feel* something's wrong. Understand?

This is about me.

And now ... the focus is on **what was said.**

No tie today? Huh. Why aren't you wearing a tie? What's with the *No tie today* quip?

The focus is now on critiquing *what was said.* The **factual** content.

It's really important to get that. The focus is quickly on critiquing the factual content. *What did he just say? What does that mean? What did he mean by that?*

It's focusing on what was said.

You are now focusing on the facts. The content. And the veracity of that content.

And you may even be gearing up for a challenge. A spar. A fight.

And when you do that **people become objects.** They become objectified. You see suddenly see them as the enemy. Opponents. Sources of annoyance that need to challenged. Dealt with. Sorted. Defeated. Put back in their place.

It becomes about power.

I am right. You are wrong.

Winners. Losers.

And now it's about defending the castle. The drawbridge comes up. Or, release the hounds. Call out the army. Send in the riot police.

To whatever degree it is becoming more adversarial. Combative.

You can *feel* it.

Why do I know this? Why am I so sure of this? Because this was me! Guilty as charged! I had so many conversations, that focused on *cross-examining* **What was said.** That were about scrutinising the **factual content.** And defending points of order. And challenging facts. And debating. And point scoring.

Just like in court.

How They Do It In Court

Let's take this line of thinking to the extreme. Fact checking for veracity.

Agree or disagree.

Just like we see in court.

If you actually worked with judges, magistrates, attorneys, barristers, lawyers, whatever, here's how they were trained to respond to any statement that they hear:

- Is it true?

- Is it false?

- Is it questionable?

In court, a barrister will hear a testimony and consider:

- Is what this person saying true?

- Is it false?

- Is it questionable? (Questionable means there's an element of truth in it that may need to be explored with regard to either a conviction or mitigating the conviction.)

My colleague works as a magistrate and is constantly listening carefully to evidence and asking herself:

- Is what I'm hearing true?

- Is what this person saying false?

- Is it or questionable?

Let's say that you're the prosecution and somebody is in the witness box and they make a statement. You will critique the statement by considering

- Is what I'm hearing true?

- Is what the person saying false?

- Or is it or questionable?

Call whatever they are saying X. *Is X true? False? Or questionable?* And: if X is true, what makes it true? (Or false? Or questionable?)

Basically, the rules of cross examination are geared towards testing the veracity of a statement. If it's true ... then what makes it true? If it's false ... then what makes it false? If it's questionable ... then what makes it questionable?

Of course in most countries, the legal system requires pre-trial disclosure of evidence before a court case where both parties - defence and prosecution - have had time to carefully review the evidence, potential testimonies, arguments so they can pick it apart and view it from their representational perspective ... and argue the case.

I'm glad we have this system because in most instances, despite what you see in movies and on TV, on the balance, justice tends to be served.

Is what I'm hearing true, false or questionable?

My magistrate friend would say, so far I am reasonably correct from her legal perspective.

So I'm in a conversation ... and I hear something that sounds and feels like a problem ... and it registers *This is about me* ... and I'm now thinking, *What are the facts? Is that true? Is it false? Is it questionable?*

And if what I'm hearing is true, then what makes it true? And if it's false, what makes it false? And if it's questionable, what makes it questionable?

It's now important to consider the evidence before you. The factual content.

But all that has an energy you can feel. You feel challenged. Offended. Stunned. Surprised. Victorious. Ready for the hunt. Whatever. Its rapid.

We've all been in conversations when somebody says something that they believe is true - or feels true from their perspective - which we instantly know is not true, or it's false - wrong! - or highly questionable.

And, certainly in court, when you watch closely, you can see how they address the facts, weight the evidence, and search for legal grey zones. Sounds true ... but let's try find where it is questionable. Or its false or questionable but let's try and make it true. Is there enough evidence to convict? Or sufficient doubt to lessen a sentence ... or dodge a conviction, entirely!

My magistrate friend says, "Certainly. You get a lot of hearsay ... *he said, she said* ... and you don't have any facts. I've sat in quite a few trials and it is apparent that the person before you is in all likelihood guilty ... but there is also a lot of questionable information. And you've got to decide: *Is there enough evidence to convict them of what they are being accused of?*"

And: Is the testimony admissible or inadmissible?

An accuser might say, *He said this, he said that* ... but you can't prove it.

So, at some point your listening has to be, *Okay, I'll hear that you're passionate about this. That makes sense to you. But it's actually hearsay.* Rules of evidence and precedent in law play a key role in sentencing.

If I watch American courtroom dramas they will say, *I object!*

They object on a point of law or precedent. They follow the rules of giving evidence, precedent. And in sentencing judges consider *Is there enough evidence to convict?*

But let's not get too sidetracked.

You're not in court. You're in a conversation. You might have knowledge skills and experience and opinions, but you don't usually have the benefit of comprehensive preparation or rules of evidence or precedent. You are right in the moment.

And that's why the potential for misunderstanding increases. But if the potential for misunderstanding can occur in a formal environment like a courtroom, what hope have you and I got?

Do I Agree Or Disagree?

No tie today?

And now I'm thinking, *Do I agree?* or *Do I disagree?* with what was just said?

And pay very close attention.

Bear in mind that the stock in trade tool in leadership coaching is *awareness.* So I coach clients to pay attention. Notice if you get the sense that something changed, as soon as possible. If you felt it, it's a key signal to pay more attention. Especially, if you are a leader.

So I hear something: *No tie today.*

And I note my reaction is: *This is about me.*

And I weight the *facts.*

And either *I agree* with this ... or *I disagree* ... with what was said ... or what I *imagine* was said.

It now looks like this.

Words and Ideas are Exchanging

Listening
Wait! I just heard a problem!

This is about me   This is about you

WHAT was said?
Check the FACTS!

Do I agree?
Do I disagree?

Now it might not even be this conscious. But you can *feel* the change in your body. You'll *feel* it. *This is about me. There's a problem here. I imagine he's having a crack at me.*

No tie today? It must mean *something* because he said it. *Why else would he say that?*

And that demands a response: *That's not true. That's not right. It can't be right. Who cares if I wear a tie or not?*

So now the focus of your attention is on, *Do I agree?* or *Do I disagree?*

I Feel Uncomfortable

So: *No tie today?*

Somebody says something and if I sense a problem and - to whatever the degree - the feeling reaction is: *I hear a problem. This is about me!*

Secondly, *What did they just say? Is that true? False? Questionable? I need to check the dress code facts.*

And: *Do I agree or Do I disagree?*

And to whatever degree, if any of that occurs - and this can be rapid - there's definitely an element of *discomfort.*

I feel the discomfort. *I feel uncomfortable.*

Importantly, if you take it personally there is a very high likelihood that you will feel criticised, attacked, defensive and resentful.

Which potentially will lead to more disagreement, and conflict.

And you'll feel unsafe. And the conversation might come to an awkward pause ... or stop ... or, predictably when this happens to either really intelligent, clever, smart people ... or stupid people, the problem will most likely escalate.

I'm being criticised. I'm being attacked. I feel defensive. Resentful. I need to sort this. I need to get on the defensive, get offensive and attack back. To whatever degree.

It's the feeling behind the disagreement that I'm interested in. What's the feeling? What's going on inside? If you *feel* you've been criticised or attacked, then what's really going on?

That can often register as feeling shock ... and anger.

They just had a go at me! They took a jab. A swipe. Don't I know that ... . That can't be true.

Just about every professional I've ever coached can tell me about a time when they felt challenged ... slighted ... discounted ... when they shared an idea ... or proposed a solution to a problem ... and a colleague says, *No, I disagree with your approach ... why don't you do it this way, instead?*

So your colleague ... or partner ... or friend says, *Why don't you ... .*

And just like that you see a problem ... *with you.* And suddenly your reaction is *This is about me. Don't they think I have the skills? Don't they think I am qualified enough? Smart enough? Experienced enough? Skilled enough? Talented enough? Good enough?*

- Words and ideas are exchanging.

- But now I'm hearing a problem.

- And its all about me. No tie today? Why don't you do it this way?

- And at that point I feel criticised. I feel attacked. I feel defensive. Resentful.

That's what you got to watch out for. That's the awareness part.

Is there a problem? Did I just feel criticised? Attacked?

Pay attention to it. To whatever degree it shows up as a feeling. On a scale of 1-10 ... a one being a small pause for thought ... to ten being enraged and offended.

If it's a one: I only felt it a little bit.

If it's a ten: I felt it a lot. Ouch!

You can't be a little bit pregnant. That's just a way of softening it. But the fact of the matter is, I felt something. Even if it was to a small degree.

So if you feel criticised, attacked, defensive, annoyed, angry, miffed, slighted, undermined, critiqued, challenged - and pick the word that most describes how you *feel* - we can predict that it will then lead to either a disruption to the flow of the conversation ... or stop the free flowing exchange of words and ideas temporarily, or completely.

Or it progresses to disagreement. Or it can escalate to a debate ... or an argument ... or totally out of control. Because you're triggered.

And potentially, now there are two or more people triggered ... disagreeing with what's being said. And now both sides, are defending their position.

Mildly or vigourously.

Does this sound correct?

Is This About Me Or You?

My Solution Is ...

So we are exchanging words and ideas.

And suddenly you hear what you perceive as a problem.

And now *This is about me.*

And the facts don't seem accurate.

And I disagree.

And I feel uncomfortable.

And when I feel uncomfortable I will feel criticised, attacked, resentful and defensive.

And all of take can happen in a nanosecond. And mostly, it's not conscious.

And when that happens I instinctively want to move away from what ever is making me feel uncomfortable.

So the most predictable, typical behaviour I see in difficult conversations ... negotiations ... is to try and alleviate discomfort. And the most common two strategies when you feel uncomfortable is to other move as far away from whatever makes you feel uncomfortable.

So, you excuse yourself. You get out of the way. You walk

away. You leave the room. You run a mile. You hang up the phone. Your cell phone battery suddenly runs out of power and the call terminates. You *accidentally* end the Zoom meeting. Or you are brave and you call time out.

Or you to try and fix the problem. And the number one variation on fixing the problem, is an attempt to correct the faulty thinking of the other person.

There might be other responses, but those are the two most common ones.

It looks like this.

Words and Ideas are Exchanging
|
Listening
Wait! I just heard a problem!

| This is about me | This is about you |

WHAT was said?
Check the
FACTS!

Do I agree?
Do I disagree?

Uncomfortable

Fix it

So I'll generate a solution.

I'll give my opinion.

I tell them what to do.

I will give advice or excuses.

Or I'll offer to fix the problem ... *for them.*

But the key questions is: *How can I fix it? How can I solve this? Make this problem go away?*

... so I can go back to feeling comfortable.

Another option is you might shut up, close down, withdrawn and think: *It'd be a lot easier if I just did it myself.* You'll generate a work-around in your mind.

But the goal is the same: *to get away from the source of the discomfort so you can feel comfortable again.*

You don't have to agree with me, but I can tell you that in countless debriefs we see this again and again and again.

This pattern or some or all of these elements. To whatever degree. Take a moment to consider any argument you've been in and decide if any of these elements were present. If the answer is Yes, they were - and if your key strategy is to correct the faulty thinking or behaviour of the other party, then this is highly predictive of future conflict ... and difficult interactions that sting and smart long after they've ended.

In some cases, you or the other party will secretly planning Round 2 ... or revenge.

True?

Is This About Me Or You?

My Opinion

Do you know what?

You have an OPINION on *everything*. Take a moment. Look around where you are now and try to *not* have an opinion about what you are seeing ... or hearing ... or feeling.

Dirty windows. Old computer. Why is that cable on the floor? Who left that coffee cup there? Who left that door open?

And guess what?

I have an OPINION on everything, too. Just ask me.

I have an opinion about my computer ... the weather ... my coffee ... my new shoes ... how I look on a Zoom call ... everything.

Take a sheet of paper and write the word opinion in big capital letters. Just so you don't forget.

And I love to give my opinion whether it's asked for or not. Needed or not.

I know what's happening ... why it's happening ... what caused such and such ... and even what *you should do* about it.

I've seen this before. I handled this in the past. I have experience with this. *I know* where this is going. I even know where *you're* going with this.

I know what you are thinking. Before you even thought it. I know what you're going to *say* next. I know you better than you know yourself.

And therefore: I have a solution. I have the right advice.

And *I know* what *you should do* to fix it.

And if you are too slow ... which invariably you are, I'll give you my opinion. In fact, I don't even think I need to know what you think or feel.

But ...

... I've been doing that for so long ... it's now automatic.

I will tell anyone ... within earshot ... what they need to do or say.

And I'm right. And if I'm wrong ... I have an opinion on why that happened too.

Get it?

(And I'm pretty sure that you'll have an opinion about what I'm saying. Right?)

Pedantic?

This is what happens.

Words and Ideas are Exchanging
|
Listening
Wait! I just heard a problem!

| |
This is about me   This is about you

WHAT was said?
check the
FACTS!

Do I agree?
Do I disagree?

Uncomfortable

Fix it

OPINION

I see this again ... and again. And I keep observing the above repeatedly in offices and homes, worldwide. And I've pretty much seen something very close to these elements for as long as I've been coaching.

And this little run down is incredibly fast.

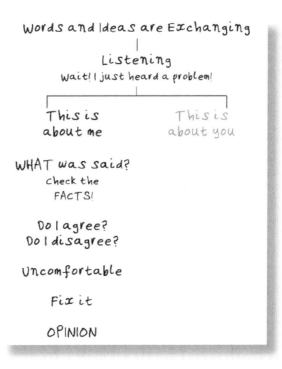

Words and Ideas are Exchanging
|
Listening
Wait! I just heard a problem!
|

This is about me   This is about you

WHAT was said?
Check the
FACTS!

Do I agree?
Do I disagree?

Uncomfortable

Fix it

OPINION

For over 21 years, I have had so many coaching conversations around conversations that turned into misunderstandings and conflicts. And whenever we unpacked what happened - especially if the interaction went pear-shaped or turned ugly - the problematic conversation followed this path.

Obviously, this is a very simplistic diagram but it shows you the key bases you'll hit in conversations that turn uncomfortable or ugly.

Conversations that leave people feeling flat. Disappointed. Confused. Stung. Smarting. Hurt. Annoyed. Resentful. Irate. Misunderstood. Worse off.

This was happening so much that we got pedantic about even the mildest of problematic conversations. Mild misunderstandings or major flare ups, this is pretty much what happens.

But once you see the pattern - in your game - in your head - when you start to see how it runs, - how it sounds - how it feels - every time - you say, *Okay, if I continue to use this strategy ... I really do know where this is going to go.*

You'll see it with startling clarity.

It's highly predictable that if you run the interaction through the *This is about me* filter - the conversation will probably leave a sour taste ... or turn ugly ... or get worse.

You'll have conversations that you're *still* thinking about ... smarting about ... hours ... days ... months ... or years later.

But ...

If you're in a discussion that suddenly becomes problematic, and you become aware of that, and you catch it in time, you can say, *Oh no, I just made this about me.* And: *Uh oh, I know exactly where this is going ... next.*

The good news is that you can pull up quickly, back track and change your strategy.

In time you get really good at identifying the elements that will run interference on good conversations - even if its a difficult conversation.

- I heard a problem.

- I made this about me.

- I focused on what was said. The facts.

- I disagreed with the facts.

- I felt criticised. Attacked. Defensive, angry, annoyed, fearful. Resentful. Revengeful.

- I felt uncomfortable. And you will feel uncomfortable. You'll try and fix it to remove the discomfort.

- I tried to fix it my way. I tried to correct the other persons perspective, faulty thinking, misguided logic ... and ...

This strategy runs the wonderful logic: *If I give you enough information you will realise you are wrong and I am right. So, I'll keep arguing until you agree ... or give in ... or give up.*

If that's working for you, keep doing it. If your interactions are amazing using this strategy keep doing it your way.

But if you've got any of those elements - and it doesn't matter what order they come in - if you've got any of those elements ... *you've made it about you.*

Recognise: *This is about me.* I'm using the *This is about me* strategy.

So take a moment and reflect on anything you've just read. Recall a recent sticky argument and see if any of those elements were present. And reflect on how that conversation went ... how it ended ... and the after taste. And then we'll explore the other column.

The *This is about you* column.

Part 2

This Is About You

Is This About Me Or You?

An Alternate Route

Let's go back to the diagram and now let's go down the other side.

Somebody says something to you. You *still* perceive what they say as a problem ... but this time *this isn't about me* ... it's now going to be about *the other person.*

You decide, this isn't about me ... **This is about you.**

When *This is about me* ... the focus is on *What was said.* The factual content. The factual accuracy. The veracity of that content. And whether I agree or disagree ... and feeling uncomfortable ... and taking it personally ... and deciding to generate a solution to fix the problem ... by imparting your opinions, advice, solutions, fixes and giving the other person the benefit of your great wisdom.

But ... if you sense a problem ... and you have the choice of which filter to use ... that will almost always deliver a mutually beneficial interaction to both parties ... then decide: **this is about the other person.**

It has to be a clear and conscious decision.

It has to be *that* intentional.

It looks like this.

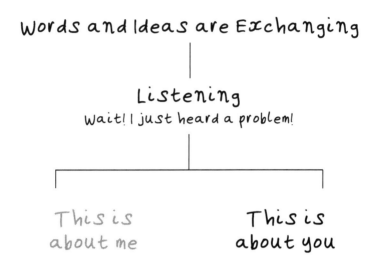

Words and Ideas are Exchanging

Listening
Wait! I just heard a problem!

This is about me   **This is about you**

How was it said?
Focus on the
FEELINGS

Now, the focus is on **How was it said?** Not on *What was said*. But *How was it said?*

And instead of focusing on the factual content ... this you time you're focusing on the *feeling* content. (As well as the motivations or values or beliefs.) The feelings. How does the person **sound** - or seem - *emotionally*?

And the key difference here is: if *This is about me,* then we treat **people as objects.** With disrespect.

However, if *This is about you*, then we naturally start to treat **people as people.** With respect.

What are you getting, so far?

Here's What's Wrong With *Them*

I often ask my clients to think of someone they habitually bump up against in a conversation.

And then to speculate on why. What's wrong with that person? Why them? What are they doing wrong? Why did it go wrong?

They usually will say that other person is *difficult* ... or *annoying* ... or *obstreperous* ... or *tangential* ... or *defensive* or *stupid* ... or a *Muppet* ... or *cocky* ... or *arrogant* ... or a *pain* ... or a host of other wonderful labels.

They will usually attribute those qualities to immaturity, ignorance, a lack of skill or experience, or qualifications.

Or, dare I say it, off the record, issues about gender, race, religion or age. In any case, the view point is either covertly or overtly derogatory ... or inferred.

They might say they have reflected on why that person is like that, but invariably they haven't reflected; they've judged. And in most cases, they will be able to explain, diagnose, describe or prescribe the other person's deficiencies and *exactly* what they need to do to be a better person. But rarely do they see the best in that person or seek an alternative explanation that involves even a modicum of respect.

Then I walk them through the two filters. *This is about me* and *This is about you.*

At this point most will confess they now recognise why so many of their interactions go wrong. They say that they realise that they *might be* - might be - at fault. They *might* need to slow down ... sit back ... pay more attention ...

Then it slowly dawns on them why they have the same interactions again and again with the same people.

Or everyone.

Understand, not *every* interaction, just those where they encounter a problem. A sticking point. Something that results in a change in the energy or temperature of the interaction. For example, it heats up ... or suddenly goes icy cold or awkward ... or difficult.

But are you starting to understand where they went? And why its not working? Where did they go? Which side of the diagram are they on? Is it *This is about me* or *This is about you?*

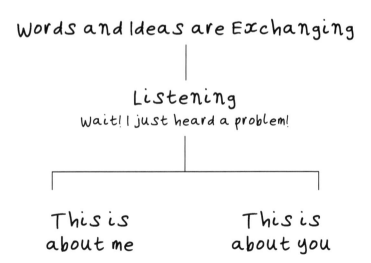

Just about everyone has someone they routinely bump up against. You might, too.

In any case, they start to recognise that they made the interaction about themselves. And they start to appreciate that they really don't know or understand why the other person is upset. Or tetchy. Or ropy.

And maybe they even quietly admit they don't care, anyway.

The more you reflect on this the more you will observe interactions and see where people go quite quickly. And you'll better understand that once someone commits to *This is about me* strategy, then it's highly predictive of problems.

If you're trying to explain someone's behaviour ... or blame them... your *solution* is to explain *why they are they problem. Why they don't matter. And why you shouldn't care.*

So again, which side of the deal are you really on?

This is about me because the word *excuses, explain, blame,* and your judgmental labels all live in that *This Is About Me* column.

And it always heads south. Always. Always towards the *How can I solve/fix this situation/person?* And almost always because the other person is at fault ... and *they* need fixing.

So the only reason you do this, is at some level, you've decided *This is about me* ... because something was said *about me* or inferred about me. And you still feel that you need to fix the other person which, trust me, lands as patronising and will further irritate the other person if not fuel their angst.

But it's still *This is about me.*

Is This About Me Or You?

Choose Again

But let's go down the other route.

Again we're just chatting. I'm listening. Suddenly, I hear a problem. But this time I decide ... *This is about you.*

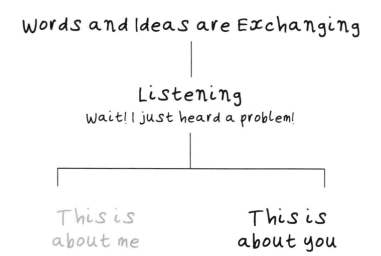

Words and ideas are still exchanging.

I'm listening.

I hear a problem.

Hmmm? Which filter will I apply? What one doesn't work?

This time the focus is **This is about you.** And instead of focusing on *What was said* - the factual content, this time I'm going to focus on **How it was said**. So, *How was it said?*

To help me better decide *How was it said* I'm going to focus on the **feeling** content. *How did they sound? How did they seem?*

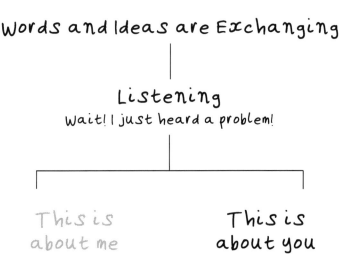

Words and Ideas are Exchanging

Listening
Wait! I just heard a problem!

This is
about me

This is
about you

How was it said?
How do they sound
or seem?

Focus on the
FEELINGS

So my colleague, Nigel, says, *No tie today?*

How does he *sound?* Seem?

He sounds or seems concerned ... worried.

That's how he *sounded.* Or *seemed ... to me.*

You're listening for the *feelings* underneath the what was said. The focus is on the *feeling content* (and I guess inferring the motivations and the values).

And when you are considering how someone feels you are treating **people as people** to be respected. **Not people as objects** to be controlled. Subjugated. Manipulated. Finessed.

So, let me just give you a quick story that highlights the key difference between **people are objects** and **people are people.**

Because I'm guilty as charged on this one.

And I learned this the hard way.

Treat People As People

I'm in Australia, and I'm on a plane flying from Sydney to Melbourne. It's the red eye. A late night flight. Not too many people on the plane at this time of night. And I've bought copy of the *Sydney Morning Herald* which I bought especially. Not because I want to read it ... but because I want to defend my territory.

So I board the plane early. The trick is to get on early. First.

The first thing anyone does is to find three seats that are unoccupied. And you sit in the middle seat ... and you open up the *Sydney Morning Herald*.

Wide.

It's a broadsheet newspaper. Big. It's not a tabloid. It's a broadsheet. So someone else getting on the plane sees you reading a big, wide open paper ... and thinks, *Those seats are taken.* And they go sit someone else.

And you think, *Yes. Job done. Mission accomplished!*

Because it means you can put the arm rests up ... and you can lay down on the three seats... and sleep on the flight from Sydney to Melbourne. Or New York to LA. Or Heathrow to Dubai. Or where ever.

Who's that about? *This is about me.*

Now, to do that, you've definitely got to see **people as objects.** Inferior. You've got to make yourself superior ... and everyone else inferior. The mindset that goes with that stunt is you actually think less of others ... and because you feel so entitled you feel quite satisfied if you manage to pull this stunt off.

And you need to think: *This is my territory. You are not coming here to invade my territory. Back off. Go sit somewhere else.*

Got it?

And you've objectified them. They are an opponent. A potential invader of my space that needs to be repelled.

That's why your key defense strategy is the broadsheet newspaper. See how strategic it is? I'll spend $2.50 on a newspaper ... I'm not going to read ... so I can get three seats... all to myself.

But there is sequel.

I learned my lesson on a plane coming back from Bali.

My wife and I are on a plane coming back from Bali on Garuda Indonesia Airlines. Flying from Denpasar Indonesia back to Melbourne Australia. And the plane is full. And we're amongst the last couple of people boarding the plane. And the hostess says, *Very sorry sir, but the plane is full. We have made a mistake. You have to sit in two different places. Separately. You can't sit together.*

She is very nice, and very polite. *And we need to find you a seat because the plane is ready to take off. We apologise. You need to sit you in different places.*

I'm having *none* of that.

No. I'm not sitting on my own. Sorry. Fix it.

Sir, we have to take off. You have to sit you down.

Well, no, no, I'm not going to. Sort it out. Now.

See **people are objects.** No respect. Zero respect.

I have a problem. *You fix it.*

So we're standing in the doorway of the plane doing the Mexican standoff.

I paid for my ticket. I want to sit with my wife. I'm the customer. My way or the highway. All that heavy self-centred entitlement sort of stuff ... getting moment-by-moment more upset. More worked up. More stubborn.

And then ... from out of nowhere, this lady stands up a couple of seats back and says, *Excuse me, miss. I have a vacant seat next to me and I'm traveling on my own. They can sit here if you like and I'll go sit in one of those other seats.*

How did she see this situation? She must have seen a couple that wanted to sit together. (A rude husband ... and an embarrassed wife.)

Her frame of reference was: **Treat people as people.**

That facts are: The airline *had* made a mistake. The plane *was* ready to take off. You *can't* sit with your wife.

That's it. End of. These are the facts.

The lady must have considered, *How do these people sound? They seem upset. They seem angry. Tired. Distressed. I've got a seat. I can offer to do something about this.*

So she said, *Excuse me.* She moved into the aisle with her hand luggage ... my wife and I sat down ... (and a very nice seat too, with good leg room) and the hostess escorted her to a new seat.

Now I know that the seat she got was down the back of the plane. Not very nice down there. But we're now sitting at the front of the plane ... with lots of leg room ... and you know what I'm thinking? *Great outcome.*

It's a long flight back to Australia. Eleven hours.

But then I'm sitting there ... and I have a long time to reflect on what just happened.

What just happened here?

And I really thought about it. I thought, *Why did that happen?* And: *Why do I feel guilty about this outcome?*

And then I realised, *Oh, because every time you get on a plane ... all you do is think about yourself.*

Suddenly I had a realisation. It all fell into place.

I wish I knew the woman's name. I really do. She became my teacher. My mentor. The lesson I learned was phenomenal. Elegant. Life changing.

I got it. **People are people.** Not objects.

Her consideration of others resolved the situation quickly. The hostess was really, really happy. Then I felt like a selfish, self-entitled tosser for getting so upset and cranky. And being so self-centred and egotistical.

I later said to an air hostess, *Can I please buy this woman something nice from you gift shop and send it back to her?*

Unfortunately, the new hostess wasn't aware of the situation ... or who the lady was.

So I thought, *How do I fix this? How can I honour this?*

Next time I'm on a plane ... or I'm on a train ... or I'm on a bus ... and there's a problem ... and I can help ... and treat *people as people,* I'm going to do that. I'm going to treat *people as people.*

When I replayed the scenario in my mind I realised that she had taken a problematic interaction and resolved it masterfully. So I started to treat my interactions in the same manner. (Now, I am not a black belt in this by any stretch but on the balance I can recognise a stressful interaction and handle it with greater respect.

I can tell you that I work with people under a lot of pressure and treating *people as people* works.

And as I started doing more of it, I got better at it.

The key is to slow the game down and give the situation and the person time. But the essence is *This is about you* not *This is about me.*

Do I Understand?

The goal is not, *do I agree or disagree?* It's **Do I understand?**

Not is that true, false or questionable?

It's *How is this being said?*

And do I understand *how* it is being said?

And your focus is: **Do I care?**

It's not about the situation. It's *Do I care about this person?*

That's the difference.

If the goal is to understand ... and to care about the other person ... then you need to take more time to be attentive ... or caring ... or empathetic ... or compassionate.

And when you do that, it tends to lead to understanding ... people feel understood ... and in my experience when that happens ... the emotional temperature stabilises - heat or the chill goes out of the interaction ... and you get better outcomes.

Your choice is to choose *Is this is about me* or *Is this about you?* You have to consciously decide.

That conscious choice tells you what to do next.

But it needs to be conscious.

Understand that if you decide to make it about the other person, it will take more time. So you need to be patient.

A hallmark of *This is about me* is impatience. Disrespect.

A hallmark of *This is about you* is patience. And respect.

Words and Ideas are Exchanging

|

Listening
Wait! I just heard a problem!

|

This is
about me

This is
about you

How was it said?
How do they sound
or seem?

Focus on the
FEELINGS

Do I understand?
Do I care?

Problem Ownership

Understanding problem ownership helps.

So my colleague, Nigel says, *No tie today?*

Who has the problem? Importantly, who *owns* that problem?

Is it my problem?

Or Nigel's problem?

Or our shared problem?

See right now, it's not clear. All I have is an ambiguous comment ... *No tie today.*

If I infer that Nigel is annoyed with me or judging the way I'm dressed ... I make it about me ...

And I can guarantee I am already adding meaning to those few words. I'm probably making it more than it is. That's most likely.

But think about it. It's really about Nigel. It was Nigel's comment. He owns it.

So, do I attempt to agree/disagree ... or do I attempt to understand? If *This is about you*, then I am going to go down the understanding route. Make that your conscious choice.

Do I understand? Do I care?

There is just one caveat. **Feelings take time.**

I need to take the time to be more attentive, patient, kinder, more empathetic, maybe more compassionate. This leads to greater understanding. I may not agree. Understand you don't have to agree.

I can understand why the kid broke into my house to steal stuff … but I don't have to agree with his behaviour. This is not about agreeing or disagreeing though. It's about understanding.

You're listening for the feeling content underneath the facts. Not *what* was said … *how* it was said.

Problem is: Feelings need to be heard. Listened to. Reflected back. And validated. Respected. That takes time.

In fact, the person and their decision needs to be respected … even if I don't agree. The goal is not to decide if I agree or not. It's to decide if I understand.

Do I understand why Nigel made that comment?

No tie today?

I want you to understand that I have picked the most benign example I can think of. *Who cares about a tie, right?* However, I have seen people end up in screaming matches over the way someone made a small grunting noise when they stood up from a chair!

See what I mean!!! He always makes that noise when I ask him to … . He is being passive-aggressive!

Psychologist, Albert Ellis once commented that New York was full of mind readers and psychics ... and body language experts. People who claim to *know* what you are thinking without any concrete evidence or support for their suppositions. People who make assumptions that may or may not be consistent with any reality ... especially in close relationships.

That outburst triggers an counter-outburst.

Look ... I've just been for a run ... I'm 46 ... I'm sore ... it was a damn grunt... ! Can't I even grunt? What are you saying? Are you saying I'm old or something?

It was a passive-aggressive grunt! I know what's going on here! It's covert? You're in your Child.

Nothing's happening ... and stop labelling me ... !

Oh really? Stop? Labelling ...?

(Now it's on. And both sides are now locked into *This is about me*.)

Has this happened to anyone you know? Personally?

Sandy On A Train

No tie today?

Nigel, you sound concerned. Or: *You seem upset. Do you want to talk about it?*

Feelings take time. If there's a conflict - or a potential conflict - it requires an **authentic willingness** to listen to the feelings *beneath* the words.

What does that mean?

It's not just paying lip service. It's actually attempting to understand the other person, especially with someone like Nigel, who isn't always direct or says what he actually means.

And, it's not being defensive. It's not trying to get the right answer. It's just listening to understand. Not to agree.

And it takes an **authentic willingness.** That's the difference. An authentic willingness to listen, not just *a willingness* to listen.

Now, I'm learning how to do this and I'm taking masterclass lessons in how to listen and understand from my five year old grandson, Sandy, at the moment.

Well, my five year old - in fact, any five year old - gets very upset about things that you and I do not get upset about.

Like busy Saturday trains on the London Underground.

We're on a train going to the London Science Museum and a lot of Chelsea football fans get on the train headed to Fulham Broadway. And it is suddenly very crowded. We're all standing. There are no seats.

And I can see my grandson getting upset. Distressed. And he says to me, *Grandpa, those people are naughty. They shouldn't take up all the seats ... and be squashing me.*

Now, normally you'd be reassuring and say, *No, no, no ... we'll get there, OK.*

But I could see him getting upset.

So, I said, *Look, Sandy, let's get off the train at the next stop. Okay? And let those people go on ahead. Maybe the next train will have less people on it.*

So, we get off the train.

Firstly, he was very relieved when we got off the train. I said, *You seem upset. Tell me about it.*

He says, *They were naughty.*

And I said, *They were naughty.*

They didn't give me a seat.

And they didn't give you a seat.

Yes ... and they were pushing.

And ... they were pushing.

And they shouldn't have done that.

And ... they shouldn't have done that.

I was squashed. And angry. And scared.

And ...you were squashed ...

... yes ...

... and angry. And scared.

... Yes.

Well, based on all of that ... I understand why you felt angry. And scared.

Yes.

And you could feel the energy changing. Shifting. He started to de-escalate. The stress seemed to evaporate. Just by mirroring him.

But, annoyingly, we had to get off the train ... and that's annoying because we were almost at Kensington ... and why can't he just suck it up ... and not worry?

Because he's five.

So, we stood on an empty platform and talked about it. (A station attendant came up to me from London Transport and asked, *Is this child lost?*

No, it's my grandson. We've just had a bit of fright on a very crowded train and we are just stopping to talk about it.

And she asked Sandy, *Is that your grandpa?*

Yes ... that's my grandpa.

OK ... just checking you are alright.)

So we had this little chat ... and I just listened ... and mirrored back what he said exactly ... and validated his experience ...

... and then he said, *Can we go on the next train now, grandpa?*

(Notice who solved the problem?)

And so I said, *Yep, let's get on the next train.*

Thankfully, it was empty and he got a seat and he said, *I got a seat, grandpa!*

You got a seat. You seem pretty happy about that.

He said, *Oh ... I am.*

Feelings take time ... and you need that *authentic* willingness to listen.

Most five years olds know when your faking it.

To be honest, it was really inconvenient to get off the train ... and active listen a child ... but I could see he was distressed. I cared about him enough ... to get off the train and find out what he was feeling. Feelings take time. And by giving him just a little bit of time ... he wound down very quickly.

So, while feelings take time ... they take *less time* in the long run ... because then he was a very happy boy once we got to the science museum, and for the rest of the trip.

But it's not something you can just apply logic to ... or give him your rational explanation.

Sandy ... it Saturday ... it's footballers ... and it's Chelsea FC. Suck it up. This is life. Stop complaining. Behave yourself! Be quiet! There's no rule that guarantees you a seat on the Underground. Read the fine print on your Oyster card.

This is a five year old. Most five-year-olds are not interpreting the world the way an adult does. You've got to try and understand it from their perspective. Even if it seems not to be relevant or logical.

But ...

How did he *sound?* He sounded distressed.

How did he *seem?* He looked distressed.

How might he seem to be *feeling?* Distressed, right?

So I said, *Gee, you seem upset. Tell me about that.*

There were too many people on the train.

There were too many people on the train ... not ... *No! Its Saturday. Its a football game. It's OK. Live with it, kid! Life sucks. You don't always get your own way.*

Sometimes you ask, *What happened?* Or *Tell me about it.* Or *What are you feeling?* You know, *What's going through your mind?*

And validate.

Well Sandy, based on all that ... I get why you're upset.

Words and ideas are still exchanged.

I'm still hearing a problem.

But now I'm focusing on how it was said and I'm focusing on the feelings underneath what was said. The goal is to understand. The driver is to care. I realise that feelings take time to listen ... reflect or mirror ... and validate (well based on that ...). But you will undo all that good ground work if you switch back to fixing and delivering your opinion.

It looks like this:

Words and Ideas are Exchanging

|

Listening

Wait! I just heard a problem!

|

<table>
<tr><td>This is
about me</td><td>This is
about you</td></tr>
</table>

How was it said?
How do they sound?
How do they seem?

Focus on the
FEELINGS

Do I understand?
Do I care?

Feelings take
time to
Listen
Reflect
Validate

HOld on to your
OPINION

Resist the Urge To Solve The Problem For Them

Let's look at the *This is about me* side of the chart again.

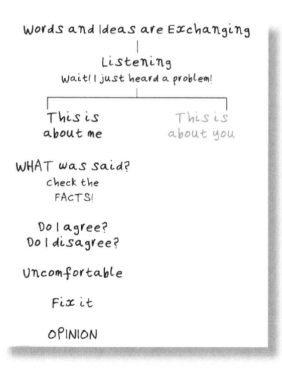

See how *This is about me* terminates at *Fix it* and *Opinion*? When its *This is about you* (the other person) you have to resist the urge to solve the problem for them.

Resist the urge. Hold onto your Opinion. Your advice. Your solution.

The *urge* is to fix.

Mindfulness gives us a technique called *urge surfing*. It teaches you to *notice* the urge. Not immerse in it

Oh, I'm having an urge to solve your problem. Just urge surf it.

Let's just surf the urge wave because the urge wave passes. The urge to solve a problem is like a wave that comes but goes. It passes. You don't have to resist it. Notice it.

Understand, the urge to fix is just a habit.

There are four options really. You can:

Fix it now.	Fix it later
Fix it before	Fix it never

Also it's about problem ownership. *Who owns the problem?*

I own it.	We own it.	You own it.

In rehab we would ask, *Who owns the problem?* Co-dependency is taking ownership of someone else's problems. And then blaming them when it doesn't resolve as planned or expect. Or it goes wrong.

And then feeling hard done to when they are not grateful.

And what message do we send when we fix the problem for others? See, you might not have to solve their problem ... or fix it ... or do anything. And fixing includes sending your opinions, advice, solutions etc.

I know you've got an opinion on what should happen and how to fix anything. Remember *opinions?* I have too. Just ask me!

In the *This is about you* strategy its OK to have an opinion ... but *what do you think? What do you think we should do? What's your best thinking?*

Ironically, the other person will usually generate the solution that feels right for them. It's likely that it won't be the right solution according to you.

Sandy said, *Oh well, here comes a train. Let's get back on the train. Can we go on the next train now, grandpa?*

So in this instance we happened to agree.

But with Nigel though, he's expecting me to *guess* at the meaning off his cryptic comment. And the problem. Which triggers the response ... *What did he mean by that?*

But Nigel *owns* the problem - it's just not clearly stated what the problem is ... that Nigel has.

He's thrown out this highly cryptic comment. But somehow if you manage to make it about yourself ... and take on the ownership of the problem ... you head into trouble.

So make it about him.

Nigel you seem concerned.

David Is Very Upset

So I'll give you the toughest situation I have ever experienced so you can see how this works. In the extreme.

My friend David - let's call him David - is in hospital. In fact, David is in hospice care for terminally ill patients. Essentially, David has an aggressive bowel cancer - and other inoperable cancers distributed around his body - and he is checking out. He is bedridden and probably doesn't have long.

So, this day I go in and see him.

Hi David. How are you today?

And the first thing he says to me is, *Andrew ... get the f*** outta here!"*

He is really ... really upset. And really hostile.

Why do you bother?!! You don't care! Why do you come in here? ... to watch me die?

Really angry. Lots of anger.

After about five minutes of this tirade I say, *David ... Look ... I don't have to put up with this ... I'm going for coffee ... I'll give you time to cool off. Sort your attitude out!*

Now, I'm pretty angry. And storm out.

So on the diagram which way did I go?

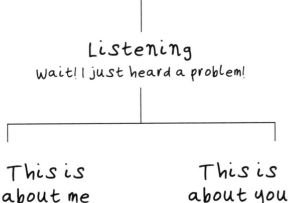

I made it all about me, right? *This is about me.*

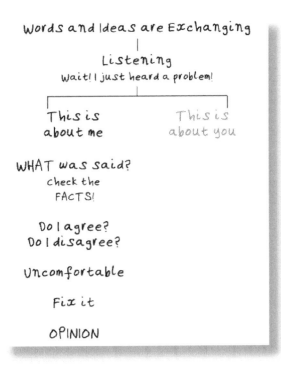

What are the facts?

Do I agree with what he's saying? No. I am definitely not coming here to watch David die. So I'm already case building and preparing my defense and my logical arguments in readiness to address that point, right there!

I definitely feel uncomfortable. And criticised and attacked.

And here's my solution. I'm going to bugger off and get a coffee. And, magnanimously, I'm giving him time to cool off. And ... sort out his attitude.

So I go down to the cafe. Stewing. Smarting.

It's a Buddhist hospice and one of the monks, Pende, comes up and he says, *Hi Andrew. You seem upset.*

I said, *Yeah ... I am.*

Oh ... what happened? Tell me about it.

OK. Where he's gone on our diagram?

Words and Ideas are Exchanging

|

Listening
Wait! I just heard a problem!

|

This is
about me   This is
about you

Oh, I just went to see David ... and he's really, super upset and .... and I'm not even in the door and he's swearing at me ... and he told me to f*** off ...

Hmmm. How did he sound?

Really super angry ... super angry ... hostile ...

Really angry ... super angry ... hostile. You seem really rattled by that ...

Yeah ... I am ... and I explain what happened some more.

Hmmm. Well based on that I understand why you're rattled ...

Yeah ... I know I should go back in there and find out what's up ... but I'm really worried that he will get even more upset ... and I'll make it worse.

You're really worried ...he'll get even more upset ... ?

Yep ...

...And you'll make it worse ...

Yeah ...

I've got an opinion Andrew ... but what's your best thinking on what to do next?

I don't know ... I really don't know ...

Can you figure this out ... or do you need time to think ... or some help?

No ... I'd appreciate your insight ... really ... I feel ... I feel ...

How do you feel ... right now?

I tell him I feel helpless. That's what I'm feeling. I'm feeling helpless because I don't how to fix David or what to do next.

The truth is Andrew ... you really can't fix this one. No matter what you want, the jury is in. The verdict is in. He's had the very best that modern medicine can throw at it. That's why he's here. You can't fix this one, Andrew.

I started to cry because he's a mate ... but also because I feel so helpless. I'm already trying to suppress deep feelings of grief ... and disappointment ... and sadness ... and guilt ... and helplessness. I should be able to fix this. And I'm angry at him because I can't fix it. I can't fix this.

So while Pende *gently* explained what was happening I sketched a diagram.

You've just had this emotionally charged exchange with David (Words and ideas)

And you heard a problem. (Listening)

And you decided this was about you. But is it about you ... or is it about him? (Filter)

And I said, *Well, it's about him ...*

He asked, *Are you sure?*

You listened to what he said ... and decided what he was saying wasn't entire factual.

Yep.

You disagreed.

Yeah ...

You felt uncomfortable ... specifically criticised.

Yes ... true.

So you decided you needed to fix it ... and your solution was to go get coffee and give him time to cool down and sort his attitude.

Yes.

And you felt ... ?

Pissed off at him. And he feels ... ?

No idea?

Do you know why he is upset?

No.

So then he took my diagram and tore away the *This is about me* piece.

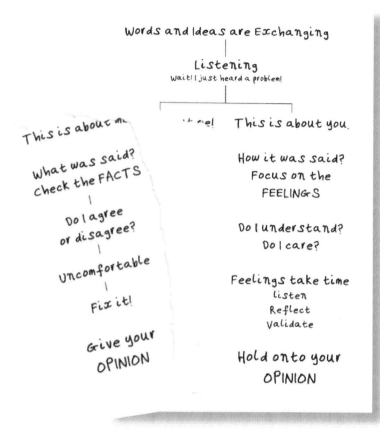

Words and Ideas are Exchanging

Listening
wait! I just heard a problem!

This is about me.

What was said?
check the FACTS

Do I agree
or disagree?

Uncomfortable

Fix it!

Give your
OPINION

This is about you.

How it was said?
Focus on the
FEELINGS

Do I understand?
Do I care?

Feelings take time
listen
Reflect
Validate

Hold onto your
OPINION

So this bit here ... is about you, right? So let's take that bit away. What are you left with?

I said: *This is about you.*

How was it said? Focus on the feelings.

Do I understand? Do I care?

Feelings take time to listen, reflect, validate

Hold onto your opinion.

Pende said: *Got it?* **Follow that path. Stick to that path.**

Thrown Back In The Deep End

He said, *Here's why it works. Do you understand why he's upset?*

I say, *I have no idea why he's upset.*

How did he sound? Pissed off.

... really angry.

He then said, *Do you understand why he feels really angry? Do you want to understand? Do you care enough to understand? This might take some time but think it through.*

No ... not really.

So, slow the game down because it can take some time. But give it a try. You know the story.

Listen

You seem upset. When I was talking to Pende, *How did I sound? Seem?*

Reflect

Tell me about that. Well I'd just had an angry exchange with a terminally ill cancer patient and I'm feeling angry ... guilty ... ashamed etc.

Validate/Support

Now you know that ... can you understand why I might feel upset? *Based on that I understand why you might feel so upset ... angry ... guilty ...*

Hold Back On Your Advice Or Solution, For Now

You might know *exactly* what is needed ... but did you notice Pende gave me a chance to figure it out?

Pende said, *That's the only four things I want you to remember. Listen. Reflect. Validate. Hold onto your solution or opinion or advice. So ... go back in there and try it again.*

So, I go back in with a cup of coffee.

Oh ... you're back. You're back! What a hero ... You couldn't ... you couldn't stay away! And he's off on another tirade.

So, I say, *Gee ... you sound upset.* I'm nervous ... but I'm sticking to the script. *Gee ... you sound upset.*

He said, *Oh ... I am upset ... . And there was a massive pause.*

Hmmm ... what happened?

He says, *Dr. Margie came in with these two interns ...* (long pause and sounding annoyed) *two girls ... two girls that are about my daughter's age ... the same age as my daughter ...* (longer pause and much more subdued) *and they're doing this ...* (very long pause and quietly) *... procedure ... <u>back there.</u>*

Take a guess. How does he sound, now? How would you

feel if young interns the same age as your children stated poking around?

Embarrassed? Humiliated?

What I noticed was just how quickly he de-escalated. The drop in energy ... that change in energy ... was rapid.

And the thing was ... he went from sounding angry ... to sounding humiliated. He *seemed* ashamed in front of these two girls, right?

I do the third step.

Well ... based on that, David, I get why you're upset.

Quietly, he said, *I am. It's ... awful ... back there.*

Now, *I know how to fix that. Tell Dr Margie to not bring those interns back.* See, I've already got that answer figured out. I have an opinion. A solution.

But then I say to myself, *Shut up, Andrew. Put that aside. Put that aside. Hold onto your opinion.*

Pende said, *I know you've got an opinion Andrew. You're a smart man. But just hold onto it for now. Let him figure it out. Resist the urge to solve the problem. Support him, instead.*

So I said, *David, I've got an opinion on what you should do ... but what do you reckon? What's your best thinking, man?*

Tools Or Weapons

Pende said, *This isn't a clever way to get what you want. If that's your intention, then David will see it for what it is. It takes an* **authentic willingness** *... all the way through.*

I've got an opinion but ... what do you think you need to do? question is a tool. It's not intended as a weapon. The intention is to **support** David ... to help himself. It *can* be used as a weapon though.

Let me tell you something.

I went to cooking classes and we were learning knife skills. But then chef held the knife two ways.

One way looked exactly the way a chef would hold a knife if they were boning a chicken or chopping vegetables. The other way looked like a mugger about to stab someone. *Same knife ... different intention.*

But I have seen people learn communication skills and acquire great tools ... which they then turn into weapons.

A client once confided that he'd done Thomas Gordon's *Parent Effectiveness Training* *(PET)*, and the excellent Dinkfus course, and excellent church marriage communication course, but I felt that all of those great tools were turned into weapons and used with almost surgical precision against him.

See, when *This is about me* your *Opinion* becomes a weapon. You use it to attack someone. Think about it. It's designed to control ... or belittle ... or disrespect someone. And it certainly conveys that message.

Some of the questions in this book are great tools ... that can easily be used a weapons. It's all in how you use them. It goes to intention. The intention is to have an authentic willingness to understand. To care about someone. To treat a person ... as a person. With respect. To support him.

This is about you ... not me.

But that takes an authentic willingness.

You can ask someone sarcastically of cynically, *What happened? Tell me about it.* And they *will* know that you do not respect or care about them or their answer.

Chris Voss, the FBI hostage negotiator talks about the intuitive ability for the other party to read any agenda or intention behind your communications based on intonation, volume, pace, and body language.

Someone like a terrorist ... or man dying of cancer ... or a five year old ... or a girlfriend ... is definitely hyper sensitive to intonation. They read your spirit of intent.

I've got an opinion. What do you think? You need to learn to use that as a tool ... or else it *will* be perceived as a weapon.

I've got an opinion. What you think?

So that's basically what Pende taught me which I then developed over many years.

He said, *I'm teaching you a tool ... not a weapon. You are not trying to control him. You're trying to understand him. You're trying to let him know you genuinely care. To support him.*

Like the lady on the plane.

So, resist the urge to solve the problem for them. It's OK to say, *I've got an opinion. But ... what do you think?*

So that's what I say to David. *I've got an opinion, Dave. What's your best thinking on this?*

He goes very quiet and after about two or three minutes he says, *You know what? I'm going to tell Dr. Margie not to bring those two interns in.*

Who had come up with the same solution? Who came up with it? He did.

Later, Pende asked me, *Andrew, why do you feel helpless?*

Because I'm used to controlling stuff. I am used to doing it my way, getting my own way ... and controlling.

The truth is 99.9% of the time, your opinion is probably correct ... and your solution's going to work.

Giving your opinion ... downloading your advice ... your fix ... is like shorthand. It works. Definitely. But people are manoeuvred around ... and instead of people being treated as people ... they are treated as objects ... where they don't get to contribute ... or buy in. It's secretly about control.

And it sends a message. The wrong message. People get it.

Pende said, *I want you to think ... in David's case ... you can't change the quality of his life. In fact, nobody can, anymore. But you can change the quality of his experience ... of his own dying.*

See in that moment David feels his life is out of his control. The situation with Dr Margie and the interns made him feel helpless ... and humiliated. He felt angry. That's why he got angry at me. Maybe he just needed to be angry. To vent that anger with someone he felt safe with.

If I download the solution ... the message is the same. *I know what's best for you. You are not in control of your own life or death. Anymore.*

But this way he's back into control of the quality of his own experience. Even though he's got no quality of life ... he's still got control over the quality of his experience ... over what's happening to him.

When you rush in with your opinion, you take away that quality of experience. You get it?

Now if he says, *I don't know. I really don't know what to do* ... is that a green light to download you opinion? Not yet. Maybe he needs more think time.

David may not have known what to do. If he asked, *What should I do?* He's given me a green light.

But you've been asked. You have permission.

Pende might say, *You know, sometimes the client doesn't know* ... and I might say something like, *How about you take some time to think about it. I've got some rounds to complete. When I come back, we'll have a chat.*

I know that when someone is distressed you can't think as clearly. You're too upset. We don't normally come up with solutions while we're upset.

The part of the brain that thinks logically, creates solutions, for example, the neo-cortex, is offline. But so is the part of the brain that encodes the solution. Your brain isn't in a receptive place for ideas and advice. Yet.

And maybe someone needs time to vent ... like David ... or Sandy. Time out to reflect, or talk it out.

Sometimes the best policy is to do nothing ... for now ... or maybe ever. Sometimes you can do nothing and that is the best thing you can do.

I've got an opinion. I'm *not* telling you to have no opinion.

When I ran an ad agency an employee might ask me a question and I'd say, *I've got an opinion but ... how about you take a short while to think about it. Why don't you take half an hour, go back, talk to you guys and see if you can kick the issue around ... and come back ... and see what you've got.*

It sends a message that you *have* thought it through, too. But it also says I'd prefer it if you think it through.

That experience was incredibly powerful for me because there were so many little lessons on how to handle the combination of problems ... and people who are upset. The hundreds of leaders who have trialled this approach tell me that it works.

But I care about David ... and wanted to be a resource for him ... as well. The concept of facilitating the quality of experience is something that has stayed with me. It's something you try and take into all interactions.

Pende   said something lovely to me. He said, *I hope you don't need a tragedy to learn that you can apply this tool ... with everybody you interact with.*

They don't need to be dying., do they?

Pende and I discussed why it is easier to apply these tools in hospitals. With people who are sick. Because when someone is vulnerable it triggers our innate compassion.

A total narcissist of course would have blamed David for being unreasonable.

I once worked with a 24 carat, gold-plated narcissist and she was totally convinced that everyone else was the problem. It was never her or her fault. When she upset her staff ... they were weak ... and therefore, they deserved the ill treatment they received. And they deserved to be fired.

You know horrible, unscrupulous, toxic people just like this, right?

Taking The Tool Into The Real World

Then I got an opportunity to try the tool out under less stringent circumstances.

I had a client, Mike, who ran an irrigation company in a remote regional country town. Mike is a real rough tough country bloke.

We got talking about his family and he confided that he had a 14 year old that he hadn't had a real conversation with for about three years.

So I taught him this system.

I don't get it. It's too ... soft. I don't get it how it works, he said.

Mike had very fast growing facial hair. When you're a coach you use what you can.

Mike, its like a four blade shaving system ...

1. Gee you sound ...

2. Tell me about it ...

3. Gee, based on that, I get why ...

4. I've got an opinion ... what do you think?

So, Mike finally gets it and agrees to road test it.

The next week he wants to share a small win.

My son stays in his room most of the time and plays Warhammer (a role playing dice game with figurines). *I went into his room and asked him what he was doing.*

Warhammer, dad ... (normal mono syllabic grunt).

Warhammer? ... ... gee ... ah ... you sound ... ahhh ... excited ...

Yeah.

Ahhhh ... tell me ... ahhh ... about it.

So he did.

Well ... ahhh ... based on that ... I understand ... why you're so excited.

Yeah ... I am, dad.

Then Mike said, *For the next 40 minutes I got the full lowdown on Warhammer ... and how to play it and ... the next night we played a game. That's the longest conversation I've ever had with my son.*

Mike's business also did welding and boiler making for the local farmers. And because they were good at it they started getting repair work for farming equipment ... and then farm bikes.

Anyway, this particular day this big rough tough farmer come into the shop and grunts, *I want to see the boss.*

And Mike goes up to the counter and he says, *What's up?*

He doesn't look happy. You can feel the tension.

*Well you welded these forks for me ... they're f*****!*

And Mike says, *Gee ... you sound upset.*

The farmer says, *I am.*

Mike says, *Tell me about it.*

The guy proceeds to tell him why the forks have been welded incorrectly ... and now how angry he is.

Mike says, *Well ... based on that ... I get why you're upset.*

Good ... well what are you going to do about it?

I've got an opinion ... but ... ahhh ... what's going through your mind?

I reckon you should weld these forks properly. And I shouldn't pay for it.

OK. That's what was going to do anyway.

So he said, *Good.* And walked out. *I'll be back ... it better be good.*

Mike's staff can't believe what happened. They are convinced the farmer is going to get physical. But now they now think Mike is a legend. *Mike, that coulda been ugly! We were sure you were gonna get whacked ...*

So I asked, *What worked?*

Mike says, *The four blade shaving system.*

1. Gee you sound.

2. Tell me about it ...

3. Based on that, I get why ...

4. I've got an opinion ... what do you think?

Mike then taught it to his team and they all start using it.

When Not To Use This

Great tool, right? Easy? Straight forward? So why would I say *don't* use it all the time?

Where it doesn't work is where someone comes up to you and asks, *Where's the nearest bus stop?*

Gee, you seem upset. Tell me about it.

They just need the answer.

So while there's a problem to solve ... there's no conflict in the exchange. There's no bad energy in it. They just need a straight forward factual answer.

Where is the bus stop?

It's just over there.

Not: *I've got an opinion on where the bus stop is ... what's your best thinking?*

Man!! Just tell me where the bus stop is!!!

Sometimes someone actually wants your opinion. This is why you don't throw your opinion away. Keep your opinion, you might need it. Don't screw it up. Just put it in your pocket, save it for later. You might need it, you might not have to use it.

Here is my big observation in working with teams. What I've found is *This is about me* actually takes longer than just listening to people, reflecting and validating what's happening and asking them to generate a solution.

Listening to feelings actually take *less* time. Feelings take *less* time. They actually take less time because you're not wasting mental energy feeling criticised, attacked, defensive, resentful, arguing, debating, disagreeing, and fending off discomfort.

You avoid that. You side step it.

You're not dodging bullets ... or explaining yourself ... or running headlong into upset. That's what actually takes the most time. Arguing with people. It's draining. Exhausting.

You get it?

But you need to prove this for yourself. Try it out.

Over To You

Okay. Moment of truth. What do you get from this book? What's your big takeaway?

I know it's a very useful tool. I use it most days.

So Nigel says, *No tie today?*

I say, *Gee you seem concerned.*

I am.

Tell me about that.

This is an important meeting and you look too casual for this important client.

I understand. Based on that ... I understand why you're concerned.

Well ... ?

Well?

What are you going to do about it?

I have an opinion, Nigel ... but what's your best thinking?

If you don't have a tie ... I have a spare one in my office that I'd like you to wear.

I'm happy to Nigel ... but can we discuss the dress code later?

And that's what happened.

But later, I asked Nigel to talk me through the dress code policy. (Ironically, the clients showed up looking casually dressed.)

But I didn't take great offence from Nigel. I didn't make it about me. I didn't take it personally. It wasn't about me.

In the past, sure, I'll jump straight in ... over react ... and think it's an attack about me ... and take it personally ...about something I've done ... or something I'd not done ... or something someone on my team's done ... and ... and ... and ...

I certainly did not make it about them ... or bother to understand ... or have a willingness to listen ... reflect ... or validate.

And of course I'd jump in with my opinion. My advice. My solutions. My ideas.

I needed to stop jumping in ... and start holding myself back ... and resisting urge to solve the problem.

You've got to pay attention to the urge to download your opinion or solution or fix or advice. This is all about paying attention. It's all about your awareness. This is all about consciously choosing a better path.

Especially when someone's upset.

That's what we're talking about.

Emotions 101

To make it super easy for you there are really two key emotions.

Upset and **Happy.**

Opposite ends of the emotional spectrum. I did a short stint as an intern in a rehab centre and they focus on five key emotions but when someone is having a melt down it's easier to stick with just these two.

Gee, you seem upset. Or *Gee, you seem happy.*

You can, of course, guess more precisely how someone sounds - emotionally. I could have said to David, *Gee, you seem angry ... or frustrated ... embarrassed ...*

He might have said, *No, I am feeling humiliated.*

In this case, you've approximated and if you're wrong the other person will tell you exactly how they feel. But they usually appreciate that you tried.

And it works for positive emotions too.

When my daughter was little she came home from school smiling ...... excitedly shouting, *Daddy! Daddy! Daddy!*

How does she *sound?*

Excited. Happy.

Gee ... you seem really happy. What's happened?

Oh, we had to sing at school assembly today ... and we all got given a book.

Really? Wow! Tell me about that.

Yes ... it was fantastic!

Well ... based on that ... I know why you are sooooo happy.

When I ran the ad agency, an artist would show me some project they were working on and I knew they were pleased with their efforts. I'd say, *Gee you seem happy.*

I am. I am really pleased. **(See how they told me a more precise feeling they were experiencing?)**

Tell me about it.

So they'd tell me how the client came in ... and they took a brief ... and they did some rough sketches ... and messed about ... and suddenly the design crystallised ... and the client loved it ...

Well ... based on that ... I understand why you're so pleased.

So, it's not just for conflict, but I developed this for leaders having difficult conversations. *This is about you* is great tool because essentially you're making it about people.

Keep it simple. *You seem upset ... you seem happy ...*

The great thing about this is if you're wrong - if upset is not the word - they might say, *No, I am not upset ... I'm angry.* Well, that is actually how they are feeling.

You seem upset.

No, I'm frustrated.

Great. They'll qualify what's really going on for them.

And then that helps you better understand how they feel.

Then *Tell me what happened.* Or *Tell me about it.* Or *What are you feeling?* or *What's going through your mind? What's going through your mind?*

That's a great question.

Oh, I was really upset about it. I got really annoyed.

How do you mean?

How do you mean? is a brilliant question, too. It opens the door wide open to share the full the story, right? To be better understood.

What if it's not the right time *for you to* apply this tool?

You might say something like, *Listen, you seem upset right now. I've got to do blah, blah, blah. But after that ... you've got me 100%.*

Or, *Can you hold that thought? I need to ... then you've got me 100%.*

Because sometimes it's not convenient for you to stop and manage people's feelings. Because feelings *do* take time.

And If the other person is particularly upset, you can say, *You sound upset ... but, you know what? I'm going to go and get a cup of tea and I'll come back in a few minutes.*

There's no rule that says you have to stop whatever you are doing instantly and deal with a conflict.

It's still about them ... but you are also acknowledging that you are not a resource for them in that moment.

Or you can set a clear boundary.

For example, when someone is ranting and raving. Or being offensive. *You seem very upset ... but I can't talk to you now. Hold that thought and I'll come back to you when it is appropriate for me.*

So little Sandy is in the garden in his sand box.

Grandpa, grandpa, come and look at my sandcastle!

I'm pruning the limbs of a tree. I said, *Sandy, Grandpa needs to finish pruning this tree ... two more cuts ... and then you've got me 100%.*

So, I cut the tree ... and then went over to the sandbox and looked at his sand castle.

Now, show me your sandcastle. Oh, look at that!

It's big, isn't it?

It is! You sound happy.

I am.

Tell me about this.

I built this myself. And then he gave me a long story about his toy diggers and his special spade etc.

Well ... based on all that ...I now know why you feel so happy.

I am.

So I'm using it on both on the emotional spectrum - when people are upset and also when people are happy.

If you really want to practice this, practice on happy situations first. Get good at happy situations.

If someone sounds happy, say, *Gee, you seem happy.*

I am.

What happened? Tell me about that.

Oh, I get why you're so happy.

Try that before you jump in at the deep end. Try it out in a more benign context.

I Wonder If You Will Try This

So, the homework is try it out and see what happens.

Pick something really benign, though. Something easy.

Mike went home and tried this out on his son ... who opened up about his hobby.

What are you doing?

Warhammer.

Gee, you seem happy. You seem excited about it.

I am.

Tell me about it.

Well, Warhammer is a game where ... look, it's easier if I just show you how to play it.

And 40 minutes later, he's had the longest conversation with his 14 year old since he can't remember when.

So when Mike comes back next week, I asked, *Did you try that?*

He'd said, I tried it out on my son.

What was that like?

He said, *It was magic. Absolutely magic.*

Mike ended up playing Warhammer every Thursday night for about two years. But he said, *We had just the most amazing conversations.*

You might be surprised at just how powerful it can be.

That gave Mike the confidence to try it out on a more difficult situation. But when the farmer came back, the bike forks were repaired to his satisfaction.

So, again, what are taking from this?

Remember especially, the filters apply once you perceive a problem. Notice if you are choosing *This is about me* or *This is about you.*

If you decide to make it about the other person ... then stay with that strategy. See it through to the end. Trust the process. It works. Don't switch strategies.

You'll notice, at first, the mental energy required to do that. It can exhaust you, but you'll find, over time it gets easier and easier.

Try it out.

And pay attention to what works. Look at the result that come just from trying this out. Just try it, but pick something benign so it doesn't feel like you've jumped in at the deep end ... or it feels too unfamiliar or unusual for you.

I don't want you to lock up.

Like any new skill, it will feel unusual to start with because it's a new skill. It's a new skill that you're trying here. I can tell you that it works, but you won't know until you try it.

You need to go and try.

Remember, it's a great tool ... not a weapon. People will read your spirit of intent and respond to that intent. If you use it as a tool - even badly, they will still appreciate that you're making an effort.

You're not beating them up with a tactic or a technique.

They still might test you ... but hang in there. So expect to tested.

And expect it to not work sometimes. Or all the time. Sometimes people are just too upset. You can always walk away. That's OK. Or you can stop mid way and say, *You know what? I am trying to understand you but I'm struggling. Can we pick this up later?*

This is a powerful relational tool and everyone who has used it, tried it, and kept using it reports just how effective - over time - it is in building trust and clear communication.

But I wonder if you will try it out?

Please let me know how you get on. Good, bad or ugly. Win, draw, lose. Either way go to *www.andrewpriestley.com* and send me a message. I get emails just about every day from people who are successfully using this approach.

And based on that I understand why they keep using this approach. So good luck to you, too!

Appendix 1
Words and Ideas Are Exchanging

Here's the full flow chart. Try it out.

Words and Ideas are Exchanging

Listening
Wait! I just heard a problem!

This is about me!   This is about you.

What was said?   How it was said?
Check the FACTS   Focus on the
                    FEELINGS
Do I agree
or disagree?   Do I understand?
                    Do I care?
Uncomfortable
                    Feelings take time
Fix it!   listen
                      Reflect
                      Validate
Give your
OPINION   Hold onto your
                    OPINION

Is This About Me Or You?

About Andrew Priestley

Grad Dip Psych, B.Ed

Andrew Priestley is a multi-award winning mentor to entrepreneurial leaders. He is a visiting lecturer at *CASS School of Business London*, in entrepreneurial leadership, the UK head coach of *Dent Global* and was listed in the *Top 100 UK Entrepreneur Mentors, 2017*.

Qualified in Industrial and Organisational Psychology he developed *The Leadership Profile* and a comprehensive *Leadership Programme*.

He has a wealth of business experience, has written three #1 Amazon bestselling books *The Money Chimp, Starting* and *Awareness* and is an in-demand paid speaker.

Andrew is the chairman of *Clear Sky Children's Charity UK* that provides play therapy for vulnerable children aged 4-12 who have witnessed or experienced a trauma.

He likes cooking, drawing and playing music.

https://www.linkedin.com/in/andrewpriestley

www.andrewpriestley.com

Is This About Me Or You?

Printed in Great Britain
by Amazon

74188856R00071